Only the Truth

by

Brianna Tate

Copyright © 2018 Brianna Tate

All rights reserved. No part of this publication may be reproduced, distributed, or transmitted in any form or by any means, including photocopying, recording, or other electronic or mechanical methods, without the prior written permission of the publisher, except in the case of brief quotations embodied in critical reviews and certain other noncommercial uses permitted by copyright law.

ISBN-13: 978-1-7320846-9-8

Liberation's Publishing LLC
West Point, Mississippi
www.liberationspublishing.com

Contents

Change 5

Why 6

Can You Hear My Cry 7

Goodbye Old Me 8

The Depression Stage 10

The Storm Has Ended 11

Who I am 12

Plus Size Beauty Queen 13

It's Working For Me, And It Will Do The Same For You 14

Forgiveness 15

I Am Not What Made Me 16

My Bully Story 17

Thank You 18

The Harassment 19

The Storm 20

The Relationship 21

You Can't Break Me 22

What's My Purpose? 23

Only The Truth 24

Change

I'm afraid of change yet I wish for change to come

But if change was to happen will I run from?

A change of a hope and a change of a dream

A change to understand what does my purpose mean

A change to know that I could overcome

And change to find out that God is not done.

Not done with my blessings or continuing my truth

This is just my beginning, my change is happening

I'm not finished yet; this change is my truth.

Why

Why is the question I would always ask?

Why me lord? Why did you choose me for this task?

I learned to not question and to let things be

I could never could understand why lord,
why is this happening to me?

Maybe he found favor in you is what I was always told

Why find favor in me? I'm just a sinner with a lost soul

Look at me now, I'm a living testimony

That God gives his strongest people the toughest battles

And then we tell how we made it, that's what we tattle.

I thank you Lord because I could've been laying in my grave

Now my biggest question is Why? Why not give him his praise?

Can You Hear My Cry

I'm just a child, they say I would never understand

Why what happened to me would soon hit the fan

They said don't worry I know you been hurt

This is my cry out, I don't want to take this to the dirt.

Somebody help! somebody help me please!

All the hurt I'm feeling would soon be released.

Can you hear my cry? Can you relate to my story?

No one else is here except me, you and God's glory.

I need to tell this. My story must be told

But how could I tell this lord knows I'm not that bold

Yet listen to what I say and what I speak

Not only is this my truth, but this is my testimony.

Goodbye Old Me

Best of luck to the girl I used to be

She's far gone and it's no turning back.

Now let's applaud the young woman I am today

She's always here and forever here to stay

Now let's thank God for how far she has overcome

But she's still striving to hear the words "well done"

When they see her they stop and smile her way

Loving the woman she has become today

It wasn't an easy thing, but with God she stayed strong

Through deaths and sicknesses, she found God as a backbone

Friends she thought she had were never still

And the loneliness she felt was sure to kill

But to glory she found a friend, a friend who would never leave her side.

When the time comes to go, she's got her ticket, she's going to ride

If you ask who might this young woman be?

Her name is Brianna Tate, and that young woman is me.

The Depression Stage

I felt alone, I felt like no one cared

I felt like if I told my story who would care what I shared.

Nobody knew what I was going through, nobody listened

They thought all my problems had ended

I thought maybe I should take my life

They wouldn't care anyway

Little did I know there was angel watching me everyday

I laid every night crying from a dream

Of a little girl being abused from the looks it seem

But that angel reminded me that the storm was only for a while

A little while to never became the reason I smiled

The Storm Has Ended

Now it's getting to my favorite part where we come and meet again

To tell our story of the storm that has come to an end

It was seasonal, and our angel told us so

Now let me tell you how I made it over just so you can know

I did a lot of crying and praying, a lot of long talks with God

A lot of walking the halls at night, praying for the safety of my loved ones.

Through his goodness and mercy, I shed a lot of tears

Praying to God, thanking him for multiplying my years

If you do the same, your storm will grow weaker day by day

And you'll come back and testify your storm has gone away

Who I am

I wrote a lot about what happened, but not enough about me

I'm the angel who smiles when people are happy as can be

I could light up a room just by the way I smile

Never rude, mean, vicious or vile

I love to encourage, to strengthen, and teach to be bold

Crazy thing I'm just learning how to be all of those

But I'm strong, black, and I will succeed

Well that's just a little black girl magic in me

I am courageous and no I'm not perfect

But if you take my hand you'll see I'm very much worth it

Plus Size Beauty Queen

I'm not your average beauty queen

I'm a plus size diva, but all they think is that I'm mean

Yet, I walk with my head held high

And I fight all insecurities because

I am grace and favor from head to feet

I'm not a size two or four, I'm a size sixteen

But let me remind you, I'm the plus size beauty queen

I won't put my head down that makes my crown fall

I'm only 5"2 but I'm the best beauty queen of them all

Not only am I the short, brilliant little black girl

I'm the plus size beauty queen who's changing the world!

It's Working For Me, And It Will Do The Same For You

I learned to stop questioning God, and let him have his way

I learned to put him first and acknowledge him every day

It's okay to stand out its okay to be different

Because when God is in it no man can end it

He's working it for my good, and I still believe

It'll do the same for you too don't move until he

Is finished working it for you, and working it for your good

Once he's finished you'll see things clearly, that you never understood

Don't give up and don't give in

He's doing it for us, new blessings for us will begin

Forgiveness

I learned to forgive others for all the hurt they may have done

I learned to forgive and to stop running from

Running from my truth and my life

And to turn everything over and make things right

I learned that forgiveness starts with me first and then others

If I can't forgive myself then how will I turn to others

No matter what they did I still love them my fellow sisters and brothers

We all make mistakes so who am I to judge

Once you forgive there's a love there that just won't budge.

Forgive

I Am Not What Made Me

My situations, yes, I may have had them but they do not define me

I am who I am because God found something in me

He used my mistakes and he worked them for my good

I'm no longer here wondering "Lord what if I would?"

My problems may have bent me, but it sure didn't break me

It only inspired me to be better than I could be

I am not what made me, I'm stronger and wiser

I am tied into love and affection, God wrap me in your arms a little tighter.

My Bully Story

Have I been bullied? The answer is yes, I have.

They say it's a child's worst nightmare,

well let's just say mines is split in half

From the torment about my weight to the torment about my hair

To the torment of my height there was no one there

No one except me, my bullies, and my fear

No one wanted to listen, no one wanted to hear

I started to cry and begin to ask why was this my life

Little did I know it was just a season to make things right

I can never thank my bullies enough for all the picking they did

My life turned and it'll my bullies never win,

Thank You

Thank you for hurting me, thank you for the pain you caused

Thank you for the drama, thank you for the answers never solved

It's not every day where I can stand proud and say

Thank you for all the hurt you did, and troubles you brought my way

To my old friends, thank you for breaking my trust

It brought to me lifelong friends, your friendship is now dust

To my ex-boyfriend thank you belittling me

Because of you I'm stronger than I can ever be

Thank you for the mental abuse and the scar

Thank you for breaking me down so someone else could rebuild my heart

Thank you, God, for never leaving when everyone else turned away

It's a blessing in every single way and every single day

The Harassment

"Stop"! "Please I promise I won't tell"

"Just let me go, this is something I can just say I fell"

I'm crying out I'm only 11 years old

When I'm older I'll make sure this story is told

Leave me alone, you're my second protector

You're hurting me, you are not my dissector

You broke me, and you took something that was precious

The first thing you told me to never give away

Lord please let me make alive to speak my truth to this one day

No weapon formed against me shall prosper is what I silently prayed

Wishing there was someone who come and save..

Brianna Tate

The Storm

Man was this a rough time and a rough patch

This was something worse than a near heart attack

Its' where I thought my life would never get better

But here I stand to say I made it through the stormy weather

Listen when I say this only so clearly

Life has a way of making things dark and weary

The storm was only seasonal it will soon come to pass

I made it out I thank God that it didn't last

My tears were heavy I didn't know which way to go

Until I heard a voice that said "you'll listen like I told you so"

The Relationship

Young and in love and happily ever after is what I thought we would be

A lot of broken promises and empty dreams told to me

He said "don't worry I'll be the man of your dreams"

Little did I know he was an enemy who I feared in my dreams

See they say the enemy wears sheep-clothing

Well he wore some that was more open and closing

He wore my heart on him because it ran so heavy

And he stomped and threw it ran over it with his Chevy

He hurt me in ways unexplainable to imagine

But there I was young and I love it was much more than I could fathom

Brianna Tate

You Can't Break Me

You threw sticks, and yes you hid your hands

You tried to make my joy and put more than I could stand

I have friend who will never leave my side

And with him I could do anything, anything better than my pride

When you told me that I could never be there he was sitting to right

Saying my child, you're stronger than this, you'll make it through this fight

You hurt me that it is true, true indeed but,

I wear this smile every day because you didn't break me

What's My Purpose?

I found myself asking this question every night

What's my meaning? What's my purpose to life

Then I began to think, it could've been worse

And then I realize that this is my purpose

To help someone who's going through the same situations

I made it out, and found my voice, now I want to help

This is only my truth, to let others know he never fails

Brianna Tate

Only The Truth

I admit I been through a lot of things in my life

I made a lot of mistakes and sometimes I had to sacrifice

I've been beat, I've been torn and broken

But I found it as a blessing of a token

If I wasn't for the shaking I would've never been ready for what it was making.

If it wasn't for the beatings, I would've never knew what my story would be

I found this as my breakthrough my change point and a turning point of my life

This only the truth, this is only right

                Only The Truth

Brianna Tate

www.ingramcontent.com/pod-product-compliance
Lightning Source LLC
Chambersburg PA
CBHW060345080526
44584CB00013B/924